CREATED FOR

Greater Things

CREATED FOR

Greater Things

JEFFREY R. HOLLAND

DESERET
BOOK

SALT LAKE CITY, UTAH

Library of Congress Cataloging-in-Publication Data
Holland, Jeffrey R., 1940–
   Created for greater things / Jeffrey R. Holland.
      p. cm.
   Includes bibliographical references.
   ISBN 978-1-60641-940-3 (hardbound : alk. paper)
   1. Holland, Jeffrey R., 1940—Quotations.   2. The Church of Jesus Christ of Latter-day Saints—
Doctrines.   3. Mormon Church—Doctrines.   I. Title.
   BX8609.H65 2011
   289.3092—dc22

                          2010044124

Printed in the United States of America
Inland Graphics, Menomonee Falls, WI

10   9   8   7   6   5   4   3   2   1

I believe we have all been created for greater things than we can comprehend.

The times call for great things, but great things

in the noblest and most redemptive sense

are predicated upon tolerance, love, respect,

understanding, dignity, prayer, God.

Be a woman of Christ.

CHERISH YOUR ESTEEMED PLACE IN THE SIGHT OF GOD.

HE NEEDS YOU. THIS CHURCH NEEDS YOU.

THE WORLD NEEDS YOU. *A woman's abiding trust in God and unfailing devotion to things of the Spirit have always been an anchor when the wind and the waves of life were fiercest.*

If we constantly focus on the stones

in our mortal path, we will almost

surely miss the beautiful flower or

cool stream provided by a loving

Father who outlined our journey.

Some blessings come soon, some come late,

and some don't come until heaven; but for those who

embrace the gospel of Jesus Christ, they come.

*W*hoever you are and wherever you find yourself as you seek your way in life, I offer you "the way, the truth, and the life" (John 14:6). Wherever else you think you may be going, I ask you to "come unto Him" as the imperative first step in getting there, in finding your individual happiness and strength and success.

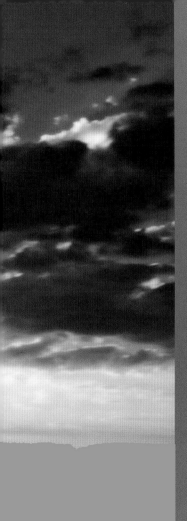

NO ONE OF US IS LESS TREASURED OR CHERISHED OF GOD THAN ANOTHER. *I testify that He loves each of us—* INSECURITIES, ANXIETIES, POOR SELF-IMAGE, AND ALL. HE DOESN'T MEASURE OUR TALENTS OR OUR LOOKS; HE DOESN'T MEASURE OUR PROFESSIONS OR OUR POSSESSIONS. *He cheers on every runner, calling out that the race is against sin, not against each other.*

GOD DOESN'T CARE NEARLY AS MUCH ABOUT WHERE
YOU HAVE BEEN AS HE DOES ABOUT WHERE YOU ARE
AND, WITH HIS HELP, WHERE YOU ARE WILLING TO GO.

Everything in the gospel teaches us that we can change if we need to, that we can be helped if we truly want it, that we can be made whole, whatever the problems of the past.

I AM CONVINCED THAT MISSIONARY WORK IS

NOT EASY BECAUSE SALVATION IS NOT A CHEAP

EXPERIENCE. SALVATION NEVER WAS EASY. WE

ARE THE CHURCH OF JESUS CHRIST, THIS IS THE

TRUTH, AND HE IS OUR GREAT ETERNAL HEAD.

HOW COULD WE BELIEVE IT WOULD BE EASY FOR

US WHEN IT WAS NEVER, EVER EASY FOR HIM?

Our children take their flight into the future with our thrust and with our aim. And even as we anxiously watch that arrow in flight and know all the evils that can deflect its course after it has left our hand, nevertheless we take courage in remembering that the most important factor in determining that arrow's destination will be the stability, strength, and unwavering certainty of the holder of the bow.

17

On that very night, the night of the greatest suffering that has ever

taken place in the world or that ever will take place, the Savior said,

"PEACE I LEAVE WITH YOU, MY PEACE

I GIVE UNTO YOU. . . . LET NOT YOUR HEART

BE TROUBLED, NEITHER LET IT BE AFRAID"

(John 14:27).

I submit to you, that may be one of the Savior's commandments that is, even in the hearts of otherwise faithful Latter-day Saints, almost universally disobeyed; and yet I wonder whether our resistance to this invitation could be any more grievous to the Lord's merciful heart.

He hears

YOUR FATHER IN HEAVEN KNOWS YOUR NAME

AND KNOWS YOUR CIRCUMSTANCE.

your prayers.

HE KNOWS YOUR HOPES AND DREAMS, INCLUDING

YOUR FEARS AND FRUSTRATIONS. AND HE KNOWS

WHAT YOU CAN BECOME THROUGH FAITH IN HIM.

*With any major decision there are cautions
and considerations to make, but once there
has been illumination, beware the temptation
to retreat from a good thing. If it was right
when you prayed about it and trusted it and
lived for it, it is right now.*

There is not a single loophole or curveball or open trench to fall into for the man or woman who walks the path that Christ walks. When He says, **"COME, FOLLOW ME"** (Luke 18:22), He means that He knows where the quicksand is and where the thorns are and the best way to handle the slippery slope near the summit of our personal mountains. He knows it all, and He knows the way. **HE IS THE WAY**.

In seeking true peace

some of us need to improve what has to be improved,

confess what needs to be confessed,

forgive what needs to be forgiven,

and forget what should be forgotten in order that

serenity can come to us.

It seems the door to permissiveness, the door to lewdness and vulgarity and obscenity swings only one way. It only opens farther and farther; it never seems to swing back. Individuals can choose to close it, but it is certain, histori-cally speaking, that public appetite and public policy will not close it. No, in the moral realm the only real control you have is self-control.

When you are confronted with challenges that are difficult to conquer or you have questions arise, the answers to which you do not know, hold fast to the things you do know.

Hang on to your firmest foundation, however limited that may be, and from that position of strength face the unknown.

He has, He reminds us, "graven thee upon

the palms of my hands" (1 Nephi 21:16). *Considering*

the incomprehensible cost of the Crucifixion,

Christ is not going to turn His back on us now.

If for a while the harder you try, the harder it gets,

take heart.

So it has been with the best

people who ever lived.

Someone you know is carrying a spiritual or physical or emotional burden of some sort, or some other affliction drawn from life's catalog of a thousand kinds of sorrow. In the spirit of Christ's first invitation to His twelve Apostles, jump into this work. Help people. Heal old wounds and try to make things better.

One would truly need a great and spacious makeup kit to compete with beauty as portrayed in media all around us. Yet at the end of the day there would still be those "in the attitude of mocking and pointing their fingers" as Lehi saw (1 Nephi 8:27) because however much one tries in the world of glamour and fashion, it will never be glamorous enough.

True love

blooms when we care more about another person than we care about ourselves. That is Christ's great atoning example for us, and it ought to be more evident in the kindness we show, the respect we give, and the selflessness and courtesy we employ in our personal relationships.

Even if you cannot always see that silver lining on your clouds, God can, for He is the very source of the light you seek. He does love you, and He knows your fears. He hears your prayers. He is your Heavenly Father, and surely He matches with His own the tears His children shed.

Think the best of each other,

especially of those you say you love.

Assume the good and doubt the bad.

We don't want God to remember our sins, so there is something fundamentally wrong in our relentlessly trying to remember those of others.

IF YOU ARE LONELY, PLEASE KNOW

YOU CAN FIND *comfort*.

IF YOU ARE DISCOURAGED,

PLEASE KNOW YOU CAN FIND

hope. IF YOU ARE POOR IN

SPIRIT, PLEASE KNOW YOU CAN BE

strengthened. IF YOU FEEL

YOU ARE BROKEN, PLEASE KNOW

YOU CAN BE *mended*.

47

For a celestial reward, it is absolutely essential that we remain faithful to the end. There is nothing in the Church that is directed toward the telestial or terrestrial kingdoms. For us it is a celestial goal every step of the way.

Jesus said in His most remarkable sermon ever:

"For if ye love them which love you, what reward have ye? do not even the publicans the same? And if ye salute your brethren only, what do ye more than others? do not even the publicans so?"

(Matthew 5:46–47).

I make an appeal for us to reach beyond our own contentment, to move out of our own comfort and companion zones, to reach those who may not always be so easy to reach. If we do less, what distinguishes us from the biblical publican?

On occasions, global or personal, we may feel we are distanced from God, shut out from heaven, lost, alone in dark and dreary places. Often enough that distress can be of our own making, but even then the Father of us all is watching and assisting. And always there are those angels who come and go all around us, seen and unseen, known and unknown, mortal and immortal.

Love makes us instinctively reach out to God and other people. Lust, on the other hand, is anything but godly and celebrates self-indulgence. Love comes with open hands and open heart; lust comes with only an open appetite.

JESUS HAS CHOSEN, EVEN IN A RESURRECTED, OTHERWISE PERFECTED BODY, TO RETAIN FOR THE BENEFIT OF HIS DISCIPLES THE WOUNDS IN HIS HANDS AND IN HIS FEET AND IN HIS SIDE—SIGNS, IF YOU WILL, THAT PAINFUL THINGS HAPPEN EVEN TO THE PURE AND THE PERFECT; SIGNS, IF YOU WILL, THAT PAIN IN THIS WORLD IS NOT EVIDENCE THAT GOD DOESN'T LOVE YOU; SIGNS, IF YOU WILL, THAT PROBLEMS PASS AND HAPPINESS CAN BE OURS.

EXCELLENCE DOES NOT COME EASILY OR QUICKLY—

an excellent education does not, a successful mission does

not, a strong, loving marriage does not, rewarding personal

relationships do not. It is simply a truism that nothing very

valuable can come without significant sacrifice, effort, and

patience on our part.

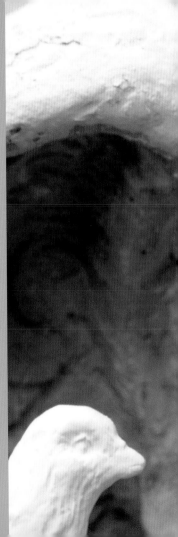

When we speak of those who are instruments in the hand of God, we are reminded that not all angels are from the other side of the veil. Some of them we walk with and talk with— here, now, every day. Some of them reside in our own neighborhoods. Some of them gave birth to us, and in my case, one of them consented to marry me. Indeed heaven never seems closer than when we see the love of God manifested in the kindness and devotion of people so good and so pure that *angelic* is the only word that comes to mind.

I suppose it goes without saying that negative speaking so often flows from negative thinking about ourselves. We see our own faults, we speak—or at least think—critically of ourselves, and before long that is how we see everyone and everything. No sunshine, no roses, no promise of hope or happiness. Before long we and everybody around us are miserable.

God wants us to be stronger than we are—

more fixed in our purpose, more certain of

our commitments, eventually needing less

coddling from Him, showing more willing-

ness to shoulder some of the burden of His

heavy load. In short, He wants us to be

more like He is and, if you haven't noticed,

some of us are not like that yet.

On this upward and sometimes hazardous journey, each of us meets our share of daily challenges. If we are not careful, as we peer through the narrow lens of self-interest, we may feel that life is bringing us more than our fair share of trials—that somehow others seem to be getting off more lightly.

But the tests of life are tailored for our own best interests, and all will face the burdens best suited to their own mortal experience. In the end we will realize that God is merciful as well as just and that all the rules are fair. We can be reassured that our challenges will be the ones we needed, and conquering them will bring blessings we could have received in no other way.

You and I won't ever find ourselves

on that cross, but we repeatedly find

ourselves at the foot of it. And how we

act there will speak volumes about

what we think of Christ's character

and His call for us to be His disciples.

Live the gospel

as conspicuously as you can. Keep the covenants your

children know you have made. Give priesthood blessings.

And bear your testimony! Don't just assume your children

on their own will somehow get the drift of your beliefs.

Please know that your Father in Heaven loves you

and so does His Only Begotten Son.

When They speak to you—and They will—it will not be in the wind,

nor in the earthquake, nor in the fire, but it will be with a voice still and

small, a voice tender and kind. It will be with the tongue of angels.

May we declare ourselves to be more fully disciples of the Lord Jesus Christ, not in word only and not only in the flush of comfortable times but in deed and in courage and in faith, including when the path is lonely and when our cross is difficult to bear.

Every day we see allurements of one kind or another that tell us what we have is not enough. Someone or something is forever telling us we need to be more handsome or more wealthy, more applauded or more admired than we see ourselves as being. We are told we haven't collected enough possessions or gone to enough fun places. We are bombarded with the message that on the world's scale of things we have been weighed in the balance and found wanting. Some days it is as if we have been locked in a cubicle of a great and spacious building where the only thing on the TV is a never-ending soap opera entitled *Vain Imaginations*.

BUT GOD DOES NOT WORK THIS WAY.

Surely there is no more powerful missionary message we can send to this world than the example of a loving and happy Latter-day Saint life. The manner and bearing, the smile and kindness of a faithful member of the Church brings a warmth and an outreach which no missionary tract or videotape can convey. People do not join the Church because of what they know. They join because of what they feel, what they see and want spiritually. Our spirit of testimony and happiness in that regard will come through to others if we let it.

In all that Jesus came to say and do, including and especially in His atoning suffering and sacrifice, He was showing us who and what God our Eternal Father is like, how completely devoted He is to His children in every age and nation. In word and in deed Jesus was trying to reveal and make personal to us the true nature of His Father, our Father in Heaven.

In a world of tribulation—and there will always

be plenty of it—let's remember our faith.

Let's recall the other promises and prophecies that

have been given, all the reassuring ones, and

let's live life more fully, with more boldness and

courage than at any other time in our history.

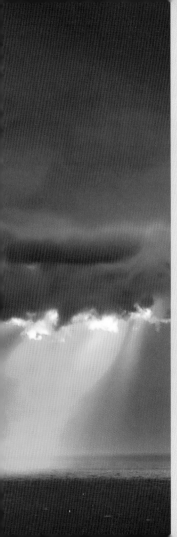

When we join The Church of Jesus Christ of Latter-day Saints, we board the Good Ship *Zion* and sail with her wherever she goes until she comes into that millennial port. We stay in the boat, through squalls and stills, through storms and sunburn, because that is the only way to the promised land.

Sometimes it seems especially difficult

to submit to "great tribulation" when we look

around and see others seemingly much less

obedient who triumph even as we weep.

But time is measured only unto man, says

Alma (see Alma 40:8)*, and God has a very*

good memory.

My concern is that you will face some delays and disappointments at this formative time in your life and feel that no one else in the history of mankind has ever had your problems or faced those difficulties. And when some of those challenges come, you will have the temptation common to us all to say, "This task is too hard. The burden is too heavy. The path is too long." And so you decide to quit, simply to give up. Now to terminate certain kinds of tasks is not only acceptable but often very wise. If you are, for example, a flagpole sitter then I say, "Come on down." But in life's most crucial and telling tasks, my plea is to stick with it, to persevere, to hang in and hang on, and to reap your reward.

WE SHOULD HONOR THE SAVIOR'S

DECLARATION TO

"be of good cheer."

(Matthew 14:27)

INDEED, IT SEEMS TO ME WE MAY BE MORE

GUILTY OF BREAKING THAT COMMANDMENT

THAN ALMOST ANY OTHER!

Fighting through darkness and despair and pleading for the light is what opened this dispensation. It is what keeps it going, and it is what will keep you going.

92

A life without problems or limitations or challenges—life without "opposition in all things," as Lehi phrased it (2 Nephi 2:11)—*would paradoxically but in very fact be less rewarding and less ennobling than one which confronts—even frequently confronts—difficulty and disappointment and sorrow.*

Teach your children that many of the blessings of the

Church are available to them because you and they give

tithes and offerings to the Church. Teach them that those

blessings could come virtually no other way.

What is the best that lies within us? Of how much are we capable? None of us yet knows. An old Arabic legend tells of a rider finding a spindly sparrow lying on its back in the middle of the road. He dismounted and asked the sparrow why his feet were in the air.

Replied the sparrow, "I heard the heavens were going to fall today."

"And I suppose you think your puny bird legs can hold up the whole universe?" laughed the horseman.

"Perhaps not," said the sparrow with conviction, "but one does whatever one can."

I suppose no one is as handsome or as beautiful as he or she wishes, or as brilliant in school or as witty in speech or as wealthy as we would like, but in a world of varied talents and fortunes that we can't always command, I think that makes even more attractive the qualities we can command—such qualities as thoughtfulness, patience, a kind word, and true delight in the accomplishment of another. These cost us nothing, and they can mean everything to the one who receives them.

*I*n such times as we are in, whether the threats be global or local or in individual lives, I too pray for the children. Some days it seems that a sea of temptation and transgression inundates them, simply washes over them before they can successfully withstand it, before they should have to face it. And often at least some of the forces at work seem beyond our personal control.

Well, some of them may be beyond our control, but I testify with faith in the living God that they are not beyond His.

A foundation in Christ was and is always to be a protection in days "when the devil shall send forth his mighty winds, yea, his shafts in the whirlwind, yea, when all his hail and his mighty storm shall beat upon you." In such days as we are now in—and will more or less always be in—the storms of life "shall have no power over you . . . because of the rock upon which ye are built, which is a sure foundation, a foundation whereon if men build they cannot fall" (Helaman 5:12).

THIS CHURCH IS THE LORD'S VEHICLE FOR

CRUCIAL DOCTRINES, ORDINANCES, COVENANTS,

AND KEYS THAT ARE ESSENTIAL TO EXALTATION,

AND ONE CANNOT BE FULLY FAITHFUL TO THE

GOSPEL OF JESUS CHRIST WITHOUT STRIVING TO BE

FAITHFUL IN THE CHURCH, WHICH IS ITS EARTHLY

INSTITUTIONAL MANIFESTATION.

In matters of religion a skeptical

mind is not a higher manifestation of

virtue than is a believing heart, and

analytical deconstruction in the field

of, say, literary fiction can be just

plain old-fashioned destruction when

transferred to families yearning

for faith at home.

If in matters of faith and belief children are at risk of being swept downstream by this intellectual current or that cultural rapid, we as their parents must be more certain than ever to hold to anchored, unmistakable moorings clearly recognizable to those of our own household. It won't help anyone if we go over the edge with them, explaining through the roar of the falls all the way down that we really did know the Church was true and that the keys of the priesthood really were lodged there but we just didn't want to stifle anyone's freedom to think otherwise. No, we can hardly expect the children to get to shore safely if the parents don't seem to know where to anchor their own boat.

I believe that in our own individual ways, God takes us to the grove or the mountain or the temple and there shows us the wonder of what His plan is for us. We may not see it as fully as Moses or Nephi or the brother of Jared did, but we see as much as we need to see in order to know the Lord's will for us and to know that He loves us beyond mortal comprehension.

Faith is for the future.

FAITH BUILDS ON THE PAST BUT NEVER

LONGS TO STAY THERE. FAITH TRUSTS THAT

GOD HAS GREAT THINGS IN STORE FOR EACH

OF US AND THAT CHRIST TRULY IS THE

"HIGH PRIEST OF GOOD THINGS TO COME"

(Hebrews 9:11).

The moment you have a self there is the temptation to put it forward, to put it first and at the center of things. And the more we are—socially or intellectually or politically or economically—the greater the risk of increasing self-worship.

We must be willing to place all that we have—
not just our possessions (they may be the easiest
things of all to give up), but also our ambition and
pride and stubbornness and vanity—we must place
it all on the altar of God, kneel there in silent
submission, and willingly walk away.

*T*hrough His grace God has dealt bread to the hungry and clothing to the poor. At various times in our lives that will include all of us, either temporally or spiritually speaking.

*Y*es, life has its problems, and yes, there are negative things to

face, but please accept one of Elder Holland's maxims for living—

NO MISFORTUNE IS SO

BAD THAT WHINING ABOUT IT

WON'T MAKE IT WORSE.

God expects you to have enough faith and determination and enough trust in Him

to keep moving, keep living, keep rejoicing. In fact, He expects you not simply to

face the future (that sounds pretty grim and stoic); He expects you to embrace and

shape the future—to love it and rejoice in it and delight in your opportunities.

When we come to worship the God and Father of us all and to partake of the sacrament symbolizing the Atonement of Jesus Christ, we should be as comely and respectful, as dignified and appropriate as we can be. We should be recognizable in appearance as well as in behavior that we truly are disciples of Christ.

*A*ll but a prophetic few must go about God's work in very quiet, very unspectacular ways. And as you labor to know Him, and to know that He knows you; as you invest your time—and your convenience—in quiet, unassuming service, you will indeed find that *"He shall give his angels charge concerning thee: and in their hands they shall bear thee up"* (Matthew 4:6).

God always provides safety for the soul, and with the
Book of Mormon, He has again done so in our time.
Remember this declaration by Jesus Himself:

*"Whoso treasureth up my word,
shall not be deceived"* (Joseph Smith—Matthew 1:37)

—and in the last days neither your heart nor your faith will fail you.

One way or another, I think virtually all of the prophets and early Apostles had their visionary moments of our time—a view that gave them courage in their own less successful eras. Those early brethren knew an amazing amount about us. Prophets such as Moses, Nephi, and the brother of Jared saw the latter days in tremendously detailed vision. Some of what they saw wasn't pleasing, but surely all those earlier generations took heart from knowing that there would finally be one dispensation that would not fail.

When Christ comes,

the members of His Church must look and act like members of His

Church are supposed to look and act if we are to be acceptable to Him.

We must be doing His work and we

must be living his teachings.

He must recognize us quickly and easily

as truly being his disciples.

We are making our appearance on the stage of mortality in the greatest dispensation of the gospel ever given to mankind, and we need to make the most of it.

I especially wish to praise and encourage young mothers.
The work of a mother is hard, too often unheralded work. . . .
Do the best you can through these years, but whatever else you do,
cherish that role that is so uniquely yours and for which heaven
itself sends angels to watch over you and your little ones.

WE BELIEVE IN A GOD WHO IS ENGAGED IN OUR LIVES, who is not silent, not absent, nor, as Elijah said of the god of the priests of Baal, is He "[on] a journey, or peradventure he sleepeth, and must be [awakened]" (1 Kings 18:27). In this Church, even our young Primary children recite, "We believe all that God has revealed, all that He does now reveal, and we believe that He will yet reveal many great and important things pertaining to the Kingdom of God" (Articles of Faith 1:9).

GOD WILL SEND AID TO NO ONE

MORE READILY THAN HE WILL

SEND IT TO A CHILD—AND TO

THE PARENT OF A CHILD.

I have beheld the power of God manifest in my home and in my ministry. I have seen evil rebuked and the elements controlled. I know what it means to have mountains of difficulty move and ominous Red Seas part. I know what it means to have the destroying angel "pass by them." To have received the authority and to have exercised the power of "the Holy Priesthood, after the Order of the Son of God," is as great a blessing for me and for my family as I could ever hope for in this world. And that, in the end, is the meaning of the priesthood in everyday terms—its unequaled, unending, constant capacity to bless.

*I*n a world of discouragement, sorrow, and overmuch sin, in times when fear and despair seem to prevail, when humanity is feverish with no worldly physicians in sight, I too say,

Trust Jesus.

Let Him still the tempest and ride upon the storm. Believe that He can lift mankind from its bed of affliction, in time and in eternity.

Fear not: for they that be with us are more than they that be with them. And Elisha prayed, and said, Lord, I pray thee, open his eyes, that he may see. And the Lord opened the eyes of the young man; and he saw: and, behold, the mountain was full of horses and chariots of fire round about Elisha" (2 Kings 6:16–17).

In the gospel of Jesus Christ you have help from both sides of the veil, and you must never forget that. When disappointment and discouragement strike—and they will—you remember and never forget that if our eyes could be opened we would see horses and chariots of fire as far as the eye can see riding at reckless speed to come to our protection. They will always be there, these armies of heaven, in defense of Abraham's seed.

Try not to compare your children, even if you think you are skillful at it. You may say most positively that "Susan is pretty and Sandra is bright," but all Susan will remember is that she isn't bright and Sandra that she isn't pretty. Praise each child individually for what that child is and help him or her escape our culture's obsession with comparing, competing, and never feeling we are "enough."

Feeding the hungry, healing the sick, rebuking hypocrisy, pleading for

faith—this was Christ showing us the way of the Father. . . . In His life and

especially in His death Christ was declaring,

"This is the Father's compassion I am showing you, as well as my own."

Just believing,

JUST HAVING A MOLECULE OF FAITH—

THAT SIMPLE STEP, WHEN FOCUSED

ON THE LORD JESUS CHRIST, HAS

EVER BEEN AND ALWAYS WILL BE

NOT ONLY THE FIRST PRINCIPLE OF

HIS ETERNAL GOSPEL BUT ALSO THE

FIRST STEP OUT OF DESPAIR.

The past is to be learned from but not

lived in. We look back to claim the embers from

glowing experiences but not the ashes. And

when we have learned what we need to learn

and have brought with us the best that we have

experienced, then we look ahead; we remember

that faith is always pointed toward the future.

Everything Christ taught He taught to women as well as men. Indeed, in the restored light of the gospel of Jesus Christ, a woman, including a young woman, occupies a majesty all her own in the divine design of the Creator.